PASCAL KOBER

# The fabulous History of Aiguille du Midi

## PREFACE BY ROGER FRISON-ROCHE

EDITION STMB - THETYS

# PREFACE

**T**he three men seemed to be descending from the sky. On the Plan des Aiguilles far below, the promoters of their extraordinary adventure followed their progress with telescopes. Would they succeed? For more than half a century, men had dreamed of reaching the summit of the Aiguille du Midi by mechanical means, but every previous attempt had ended in failure. The cable from the village of Les Pèlerins to the Glaciers had never been taken any higher; and a thin wire attached to the Col du Midi (3,500 m.), which had never been used for anything other than a supply line for a detachment of Chasseurs Alpins during the resistance, was all that was left to relate the slow and painful progress of machinery in these regions. The engineer Lora Totino, who had already erected a cable system to the foot of the Pyramide du Cervin on the Italian side, had taken up the challenge; "I will reach the very top of the Aiguille" he declared. His challenge was immediately taken up by the French ministry of Public Works, which specified that if he "stretched a cable between the summit of the Aiguille and the intermediate cablecar station on the Plan de l'Aiguille" (already completed), he would "be given the requisite authorization". To this purpose, three tough guides from Chamonix, the Demarchi brothers, were now climbing down the north face of the Aiguille du Midi, attached to a huge steel cable which served as both a safety line and a doubled rope. Undaunted by avalanches of sérac, rockfalls, and sudden rushes of snow, they gradually lowered themselves down the cliff face, while their companions above, men from the Valley of Aosta and from Venice, unrolled the two kilometres of cable from an enormous spool. By nightfall, the descent was completed. From now on there would be a link between the summit of the Aiguille and the intermediary cable-car station, and Lora Totino's wager had paid off. Brilliant exploit, or an insult to the mountain? The prize was a marvellous one: from this summit, the view of the upper stages of Mont Blanc appear in all their beauty and grandeur, a breathtaking sweep of nothingness through which the tiny pod-like cable-cars travel to and fro. At the time, many observers condemned the new cable on the grounds that the "mountain should remain inviolate. Only those who climb her on foot are worthy of her reward". Those who raised objections to the original project were among the first to use the completed "téléphérique", which is one of among the most popular mountain venues in the world. Among the thousands who visit the Aiguille du Midi every year, not one in a hundred would ever have had the opportunity to appreciate the beauty of the high Alps were it not for the cable-car and its builders. With this convenient mode of access, mountaineers have discovered difficult new routes which were previously unreachable because of their remoteness from base camp. These include classic climbs in the Aiguilles du Diable sector; new itineraries perfectly suited to sophisticated modern mountaineering techniques dependent on crampons, ice-axes, warm light clothing, and freeze-dried food. In addition, the Mont Blanc traverse could now be attempted in safe conditions. The advent of the cable-car also led to the discovery of the celebrated Vallée Blanche (or White Valley). Today, between January and May, thousands of people make the pilgrimage to this locality, where they can experience one of the longest ski descents in Europe, amid the astonishing Glaciers du Géant and the Mer de Glace. "But what about aesthetics?" say the cable-car's detractors. "Don't you think the landscape's been ruined?" Well, let's look at the Aiguille du Midi in its present state, crowned with a television transmitter which makes it look even more needle-like. You will need powerful binocular to pick out the cable-car station up there; and unless you already knew where to look, you will never catch sight of the suspended cabins as they slip along the north face on their 3,000 metre cable. But the passengers see every stage of the mountain, from base to peak; from the Plan des Aiguilles pastures, haunted by chamois and marmots, to the hanging sérac of the glacier ridges and the mighty granite cliffs scarred by avalanches. Let us accept the fact: the construction of the Aiguille du Midi cable-car has been an advantage and a benefit to mankind for two incontrovertible reasons. One, it has opened up a magical area to all comers, which before was the fief of a privileged few. And two, it has given the 15,000 inhabitants of the Chamonix valley a range of tourist-related economic activities, and these today constitute the sole commercial resource of the ancient, hidden valley discovered by Pococke and Windham in 1744.

ROGER FRISON-ROCHE

# FOLLOW THE GUIDE TO PLAN DE L'AIGUILLE

*A car arriving at the intermediate station at Plan de l'Aiguille (2 317 m).*

**Y**ou've just boarded the Aiguille du Midi's cableway to leave for the discovery of the fantastic universe of the high mountain. In a few moments, another world will open in front of you. A landscape of rock and ice where nature is as it was on its first day. But before, all the levels of alpine vegetation will unfold before your eyes. The car leaves the station (1 030 m) and begins to fly over the forest. A small hike meanders between the trees, right under the cableway cables. A moment later, it branches off in another direction because the slope is too steep. The hikers you can see climbing on the path leading to Plan de l'Aiguille will arrive many hours after you.

## Deers and marmots

Since the Blaitière forest is a hunting preserve, you will certainly have the opportunity to glimpse at animals in the wild. The deers are the kings of these woods but you can also see some stags. Spring is the ideal period to see the wildlife because it cannot hide yet under the tree leaves. After the small ridge that overlooks the forest and before arriving to the second pylon, you can see the Plan de l'Aiguille refuge on the left. The panorama on your right offers a nice vista of the Bossons glacier's seracs, the north face of Mont Blanc and the Grands Mulets refuge (3 051 m) which can be seen near a rocky outcrop.

## Climbs and hikes

Initially, Plan de l'Aiguille was a mountain pasture at the foot of the Aiguilles de Chamonix. Today, the cableway's intermediate station (2 317m) which you've reached in eight minutes is the starting point of alpine climbs and hikes to the Aiguilles du Peigne, de Blaitière, du Grépon, des Grands Charmoz, des Petits Charmoz and de l'M, after about an hour's walk. You can also go from here to the Grands Mulets refuge on the winter route to Mont Blanc.

*Right-hand page. Aiguille du Midi towering over the Bleu lake at Plan de l'Aiguille.*

# FOLLOW THE GUIDE FROM PLAN DE L'AIGUILLE TO AIGUILLE DU MIDI

■ **KAMIKAZE SKI**
It may seem incredible to the skier used to the marked out runs of the ski resorts, but almost all the couloirs of Aiguille du Midi's north face have been skied down (and even surfed down !) although some require abseiling on the rocky parts. Extreme skiing reserved for gliding daredevils.

*The steep couloirs of Aiguille du Midi have been skied by extreme experts.*

**A**t Plan de l'Aiguille (2 317 m), you will change cars and take the second part of the cableway. If you want to walk a little around the intermediate station, be careful not to venture on the snow or in dangerous spots. In the spring, if you keep quiet and unobtrusive you may see some chamois leaping from rock to rock. In summer, they will reach the edge of the Bossons glacier on the right. In the stony fields overlooking the site you can sometimes see marmots only just awake from their long winter slumber.

## The Frendo route

Just after its departure the car strides across a gigantic snow slope. It's not a névé like the ones you've seen near the station, but a real live glacier with crevasses and seracs. The funnel-shaped Pèlerins glacier collects all the snow slides coming down from the small hanging glaciers of Aiguille du

Midi and from the great cirque of the Aiguilles de Chamonix. Almost all the couloirs of the north face of the now clearly visible Aiguille du Midi have been climbed but they are rarely used nowadays because of the hazards of falling rocks particularly at the end of the season. The most famous route and still the most popular today is the one that goes through the Frendo spur climbed for the first time in 1941. Except for its lower part, it unfolds under a thin snow ridge very aerial and very spectacular.

## A beautiful playground

The cable-car passes just a stone's throw from this route. From June to the end of August, if there isn't too much ice and the route is negotiable, you will certainly have the opportunity to see a roped party hard at work, which will join you later at the summit. Just before arriving at an altitude of 3 842 metres, you will almost be able to touch the red protogine rock, a variety of alpine granite which is a little cleaved on the north face. But on the other side, the rock is in better shape and is the favourite playground of high altitude climbers which have open numerous routes on it.

**■ WILDLIFE**
Animals are few at 3 842 metres above sea level. However, on the cableway's route one can sometimes see weasel and marten tracks. And if the chamois rarely ventures at these heights, the king of the high mountain is indeed the yellow beaked jackdaw, this big black bird you will see soaring and screeching above your heads.

*3 842 meters !*
*A breathtaking view.*

# FOLLOW THE GUIDE TO AIGUILLE DU MIDI'S SUMMIT

**Y**ou disembark into the fantastic universe of the high mountain. The Aiguille du Midi's summit is a world by itself: two gigantic rocky peaks soaring majestically in the middle of the Mont-Blanc massif's glaciers. Before the cableway's construction, only the mountaineers could reach it, and by very difficult routes. Today, both summits are equipped to make your visit comfortable and secure. When you step out of the car you first reach the north peak (3 795 m) linked to the central peak (the highest at 3 842 m) by a seventeen metres long metal footbridge.

## Guided tour

On the first peak, you will find the cableway station, a restaurant, a snack-bar, a souvenir shop and the Chamonix terrace. However, we advise you to cross the footbridge towards the various panoramas as soon as you arrive. You can thus visit the north peak when you return to the departure station. If you plan a short visit, do not miss the central peak, the most impressive with the Mont-Blanc terrace offering a fantastic view of the "Roof of Europe" (4 807 m). After the footbridge, make a right turn and follow the Mont-Blanc gallery for a hundred metres. This corridor will also lead you to a lift which will bring you to the summit terrace, Aiguille du Midi's highest point (3 842 m), with its overhanging panorama.

■ **ROCK CLIMBING TODAY**
**Many high altitude routes have been opened on the south face of Aiguille du Midi. Rather short (200 to 250 m in height) but very difficult routes were first opened up by Maurice Baquet and Gaston Rébuffat a few years after the opening of the cableway. There is no doubt that without the latter Aiguille du Midi would never have welcomed so many top climbers.**

## An ice tunnel

To your left after the footbridge, you can walk to a gallery leading to the departure of the Vallée-Blanche cable-car and to an ice tunnel, starting point of the Vallée-Blanche ski descent. Here you really are in high mountain territory. Be careful because the ground is slippery and do not venture on the slope even if it is secured by a handrail. Finally, if you've decided to do the round trip journey to the Helbronner peak, we advise you to go directly to the Vallée-Blanche cable-car departure and to visit Aiguille du Midi upon your return only.

*Right-hand page:*
*On the Cosmiques ridge*
*below Aiguille du Midi,*
*climbers have found*
*a playground.*

*Following double page:*
*Aiguille du Midi as seen from*
*the Cosmiques ridge.*

# THE FABULOUS HISTORY OF THE CABLEWAY'S CONSTRUCTION

One can very easily reach Aiguille du Midi's summit today because men have expended boundless ingenuity as well as titanic efforts in order to succeed in this out-of-the-ordinary venture. The cableway's construction was a great modern ages epic. The concept is however very old since a project linking the Chamonix valley to Mont Blanc via Aiguille du Midi was put forward in the nineteenth century.

## The world's longest range

In 1909, the town of Chamonix grants a concession to a firm planning to build a cableway from Les Pèlerins (1 030 m) to Aiguille du Midi (3 842 m) via La Paraz (1 693 m), the glaciers station (2 414 m) and the Midi pass (3 555 m). The work starts in 1911, is stopped by World War I and resumes in 1923. The first section is finished in 1924, the second in 1927 and a service line to the Midi pass is opened in 1940 in order to pursue the planned work. But World War II will halt this progression. Up to 1949, the first two

sections will nonetheless welcome many visitors but, forty years after the initial sketches, the technology has advanced: engineers can now build special lighter steels and draw longer ranging cables between two pylons. The project is picked up again by a team formed by count Dino Lora Totino di Cervinia and Philippe-Edmond Desailloud. The former is a technician. A visionary engineer and a textile manufacturer from Turin, he has just completed the construction of two cableways at the Matterhorn and at Entrèves. The second, a general consultant, has a wide experience in the administrative processing of complex projects. Their idea leaves everybody sceptic: they propose to abandon the existing installations rather than modernise them and to join Chamonix to Aiguille du Midi by two sections only. Even better, no pylon will support the cable between Plan de l'Aiguille, halfway up, and the summit. The world's longest range (3 000 metres with a 1 500 meters difference in height) gives cause for anxiety. An impossible bet ? The administrative authorities are convinced of it since they declare that they will grant the concession for the construction only if a cable can be hung between Aiguille du Midi and Plan de l'Aiguille without it touching the ground. The count and the general consultant believe in their project. And they make it come true.

## An unusual roped party

In June 1950, a team of guides is at the Midi pass, waiting for the service car of the old cableway. It carries a steel cable weighting more than a ton with a diameter of eleven millimetres and a length of one

■ OBSERVATORIES
**Below Aiguille du Midi, the Cosmiques refuge (3 613 m), recently renovated by the Chamonix guides company, was built in 1940 on the physician and academician Louis Leprince-Ringuet's initiative. Scientists sometimes spent several days there to install small photographic plates on Mont Blanc's summit in order to record cosmic radiations. A number of key figures (such as Emile Allais, Maurice Baquet, Irène Joliot-Curie and Gaston Rébuffat) have stayed there. Nowadays, physicians seem to prefer the Midi de Bigorre peak in the Pyrenees and the particle accelerator of the Centre Européen de Recherche Nucléaire (CERN).**

thousand eight hundred and fifty metres. The guides rope up, each carrying by way of rucksack some fifty kilos of rolled cable ! The wildest roped party of all the history of mountaineering will take one morning to climb the few three hundred metres of difference in height between the Midi pass and the north peak. At the summit, the cable is winded round a winch in order to make it go down the almost vertical wall to Plan de l'Aiguille. Seven guides (Gérard, Paul and Roger Demarchi from Chamonix, Arturo Ottoz and Attilio Truchet from Courmayeur, Ferdinando Gaspard and Armando Perron from Val Tournanche) undertake this titanic work, unwinding the cable along their progression on the Frendo spur in spite of falling rocks, avalanches and cracks in which the metal gets caught. Nine hours later, they reach Plan de l'Aiguille. The count has won his bet.

## Herculean tasks

Immediately, a jig-back is installed between the Cosmiques refuge and the central peak in order to transport men and materials. A hole is drilled from one side of the north peak to the other, two galleries are dug in the central peak and a footbridge is built between both summits. But these Herculean tasks are not performed without some difficulty, particularly for the hundred or so men working at an uncommon altitude. Thus the cement bags, handled over and over between the valley and the building site, often arrive half full. Thus stocks of rubber bands and old tires have to be burnt in order to prevent the water from freezing and to mix the concrete in normal temperature conditions. Thus also must the rock be reinforced in certain places to anchor the installations. In spite of these hazards and after four years of work, the first section of the cableway is opened on July 25th 1954 and the second a year later, on June 24th 1955. The fabulous history of the construction had come to an end.

■ **SOME GOOD ONES...**Helbronner was one of the first geographers to draw a precise cartography of Mont Blanc. Although the scientist left its name to the summit on which the Italian cableway arrives, some of the visitors still don't know him. Thus, the cashiers hear some good ones when they are asked for a round trip ticket to the Helbronner peak: " the weekly (in French "hebdomadaire") peak ", "the helicopter peak" or even "the dromedary peak". Although it's true the peak only has... one bump !

**NORTH PEAK:**
1 Station of arrival and departure of the cableway
2 Chamonix terrace
3 Toilets
4 "Le 3842", a traditional restaurant
5 Cafeteria
6 Refreshments and "Le croque-minute" snack-bar

**CENTRAL PEAK:**
7 Footbridge and cashdesk
8 Lift
9 Telephones
10 Summit terrace (3 842 m)
11 Mont-Blanc gallery
12 Refreshments and "Le croque-minute" snack-bar
13 Toilets
14 Mont-Blanc terrace
15 Departure of the Vallée-Blanche cable-car
16 Ice tunnel
17 Vallée-Blanche gallery

# NORTHERN PANORAMA: THE CHAMONIX VALLEY

*Aiguille de Blaitière, part of the Aiguilles de Chamonix.*

**■ PIONEERS**
As soon as 1741, reverend Richard Pococke and William Windham, two English travellers residing in Geneva, explored the Chamonix valley and brought back prints of the most significant landscapes. There were thus the first to disclose the splendours of the high mountain to a general public already eager for discoveries.

*Preceding double page: From Aiguille du Midi, the view northwards reaches far away over a succession of levels, turning gold under the setting sun.*

*Following double page: Eastern panorama: Les Grandes Jorasses hide behind the Rochefort ridges.*

**F**ollow the cable. Indeed, for those of you who've lost their sense of direction, it points northwards, give or take a few degrees. In the bottom of the valley and to the left, one can first see the Pèlerins hamlet where the old cableway started at the beginning of the century and which now gives access to the Mont-Blanc tunnel. To the right are stretched out the numerous buildings of Chamonix whose actual look, shaped by history, is that of a small town. A few decades ago, it was only a small mountain village like so many others in Haute-Savoie. In line with Chamonix, one can also see the cableway's intermediate station as well as, on the other side of the valley, the slopes of the Brévent (2 525m) a renowned winter sports resort. Then the valley makes its way towards nearby Switzerland and unwinds its hamlets (Les Plans, Les Nants, Les Tines, etc.) up to Argentière. Over all these small villages towers to the north-west the Aiguilles-Rouges massif which reaches its highest point at Aiguille du Belvédère (2 965 m) and which contains a nature sanctuary.

## Here begins the high mountain

North-eastward, to the forefront and to the right of the cableway, the small Pèlerins glacier heralds the high mountain with, on the right, the famous Aiguilles de Chamonix. In order: Aiguilles du Plan (3 673 m), de Blaitière (3 522 m), du Grépon (3 482 m) and des Grands Charmoz (3 444 m). Further on, parted by the Mer de Glace, which originates at the foot of Aiguille du Midi, other prestigious summits: Aiguille du Dru (3 754 m) and AiguilleVerte (4 122m). In fine weather, the view stretches over the northern part of the Alps up to lake Léman, the foothills of Jura and the Bernese Alps in Switzerland.

# EASTERN PANORAMA: ITALY AND SWITZERLAND

**E**astward, one's gaze can leap from frontier to frontier. Although the largest part of the Mont-Blanc massif is in French territory, near by Switzerland and Italy are also mountain countries. To this testifies the Matterhorn (4 477 m) whose slender outline you can see practically due east, some sixty kilometres away as the crow flies, and which towers over Zermatt on its Swiss side and Breuil-Cervinia on its Italian one.

## Prestigious summits

But the journey to the high mountain starts right under your feet. This gigantic glacier going down softly in front of you before branching off to the left is the famous Vallée Blanche, an itinerary followed by expert skiers in the spring. More on the left, La Dent du Requin (3 422 m) hides from your view the other side of the Aiguilles de Chamonix. And this big white basin, in the bottom in line with the snow ridge, is the Talèfre glacier surrounded by various prestigious summits: Les Droites (4 000 m), Les Courtes (3 856 m), etc. When you follow, on your right, the line of ridges marking the frontier with Italy, you can successively distinguish Aiguille de Talèfre (3 730 m), Aiguille de Leschaux (3 759 m), Les Grandes Jorasses (4 208 m), La Dent du Géant (4 013 m) and its glacier and the Helbronner peak (3 322 m). On the latter, set almost exactly in the south-eastern axis, is located the station of the Vallée-Blanche cable-car which crosses the Géant glacier and passes by Le Gros Rognon (3 541 m) to reach the Aoste valley on the Italian side.

■ **FIRST ASCENTS**
Most of the summit you see east of Aiguille du Midi have been climbed for the first time at the end of the last century.
1865: south-eastern side of Aiguille Verte and south-western side of Les Grandes Jorasses by Edward Whymper.
1871: south-eastern side of Aiguille du Plan.
1872: eastern ridge of Aiguille de Leschaux
1876: south face of Les Droites.
1878: south-eastern side and eastern ridge of Aiguille du Dru. First experimentation with the abseiling descent technique in the western Alps. The Dru has become a mythical summit since the incredible feat of Walter Bonatti's solitary climb in August 1955.
1879: south-western side of Aiguille de Talèfre.
1881: northern ridge of Aiguille du Grépon by Albert Mummery.
1882: south-west face of La Dent du Géant thanks to artificial means (fixed ropes).
1885: normal route of Aiguille des Grands Charmoz.
1897: west-north-western ridge of Les Courtes.
1898: Spencer couloir of Aiguille de Blaitière
1898: south-west face of La Dent du Requin.

*Eastwards, the Vallée Blanche and the Envers des Aiguilles cannot be seen from Aiguille du Midi.*

# SOUTHERN PANORAMA: MONT BLANC

*Switzerland and Italy as seen from the Helbronner peak.*

■ After coming down from the Tacul glacier in 1788, Horace-Bénédict de Saussure will write : "The soul rises, theoretical views seem to expand and in the middle of this majestic silence, one can hear Nature's voice."

*Preceding double page: Southern panorama: Mont Blanc du Tacul, Mont Maudit and Mont Blanc.*

**S**outhward finally unfolds in front of your eyes the one for which you've probably climbed to Aiguille du Midi. Mont Blanc, great lord of these premises, towers above all the scenery from its 4807 metres. Looking left of the Helbronner peak and the Géant glacier, you can distinguish in the distance the Grand Paradis massif in Italy and the Ruitor glacier. In the foreground, here are La Tour Ronde (3 792m), Le Grand Capucin (3 838m) and the Aiguilles du Diable (4 144 m). To their right, you can see the three tremendous "steps" of Mont Blanc: the rocky spurs of Mont Blanc du Tacul (4 248 m) followed by Mont Maudit (4465 m) and finally by majestic Mont Blanc, a round bump in the background. Don't trust its kindly appearance. Although its climb is within the reach of a trained mountaineer, Mont Blanc also has very difficult routes along its six ridges (Bosses, Mont Maudit, Peuterey, Innominata, Brouillard and Bionnassay).

## A very busy route

The snowy ridge, self-evident, which goes down on the right to join the Goûter's dome (4 304 m) via Les Bosses (4 513 m), the Vallot refuge (4 362 m) and « Les Rochers Foudroyés » is considered the normal summer route to reach the summit in two days. Everyday, tens of mountaineers take this route early in the morning. It would be surprising if you didn't see a roped party or two while looking at the ridge through binoculars. Curiously, this isn't the route taken by Mont Blanc's pioneers. Indeed, in 1786, Jacques Balmat and Michel-Gabriel Paccard passed by the Grand Plateau, this gigantic shelf of ice you see just below the summit. By this itinerary, one can reach the roof of Europe directly from Aiguille du Midi. This classic route, feasible in only one day, goes down the snow ridge leading to the Vallée Blanche, over the Midi pass, up the great slope of Mont Blanc du Tacul and down to the Brenva pass before reaching Mont Blanc.

# WESTERN PANORAMA :
# THE WHOLE ALPINE RANGE

**F**rance from the sky. What greatest geography lesson could the western panorama of Aiguille du Midi offer ? On a clear day, the view stretches to the Pilat in the Massif Central via various levels of alpine vegetation. In the foreground, Aiguille du Goûter (3 863 m) first catches the eye. In the extension of the Bosses ridge and the Goûter dome, it announces the return to the valley. On it, the Goûter refuge is the first stop for mountaineers starting Mont Blanc's ascent from the station of arrival of the Mont-Blanc Tramway at « Nid d'Aigle » (2 372 m).

## An unusual face

Further on the right, rock and ice leave their place to softer slopes, forests and high mountain pastures studded with small villages. The mountain regains a familiar face but also presents itself in an unusual light. To tower over the whole alpine range in such a way is rather uncommon. It unfolds in front of your eyes from Megève (1 082 m) to Mont Charvin (2 409 m) and from Sallanches (549 m) to the Aravis massif. Beyond are the lakes of Annecy and Bourget followed by Lyon and its suburbs. Finally, in the background, right behind the last foothills of Brévent, the sheer cliff rising over Sallanches and the village of Passy is Aiguille de Varan (2 544 m). To its right, the Platé desert displays its wild rocky landscape over many kilometres. You've come full circle when your gaze comes back to Chamonix and its valley.

*At dawn on Aiguille du Goûter, a group climbers on their way to Mont Blanc.*

*Following double page: Western panorama: beyond Dôme du Goûter, the beautiful Bionnassay ridge towers at 4 052 meters.*

# AUGUST 1856 : AIGUILLE DU MIDI'S FIRST ASCENT

**A**iguille du Midi was conquered only seventy years after Mont Blanc. An additional proof that this summit is one of the most difficult of the Mont-Blanc massif. Previously, in August 1818, count Malczewski did arrive to the summit by climbing up the Vallée Blanche with Jean-Michel Balmat and five other guides from Chamonix. But he only reached the north peak, the lowest of the two. Thirty years later, another count almost made his mark in the history of mountaineering: "After hearing over and over again that this ascent could not be done, so was I determined to make an attempt at climbing this cruel peak." Ferdinand de Bouillé first tries to reach the summit by the Aiguille du Plan's glaciers, then by the Mer de Glace. Forced to turn back because of a storm, he sets out again a few days later by the Bossons glacier. Another failure.

## For the king

The following year, he orders three four metres long ladders covered with picks, hooks and crampons as well as sisty metres of ropes. He hires a group of guides and porters led by Gédéon Balmat. Going back another time by the Mer de Glace they bivouac a few cable's lengths away from Mont Blanc du Tacul. The next day, they finally see the south-western side of Aiguille du Midi. But the guides are sceptical: "It is impossible to climb this mountain." Tenacious, the count decides to go nevertheless to the foot of the face and finds himself in front of a smooth wall three hundred metres high. The real ascent begins. Twenty four metres from the summit, the technical difficulties are such that Ferdinand de Bouillé is forced to let his guides continue alone. An hour later, Jean-Alexandre Devouassoud, Ambroise and Jean Simond reappear: "Your flag flies up there, Your Lordship, but for all the money in the world, we wouldn't go back to the ridge we just crossed. Our souls may go there after our death but our bodies, never." The flag mentioned is a white banner decorated with fleurs-de-lis. We are indeed at the time of the Second Empire and the count is very proud of having been able to unfurl the standard of the monarchy on this prestigious summit.

*A roped party on the Cosmiques ridge just under Aiguille du Midi.*

*Great contemporary climbers: Christophe Profit and Catherine Destivelle.*

*Right-hand page: Mountaineering has recently seen the important expansion of paragliding. A must in the Mont Blanc massif!*

# MOUNTAINEERING TODAY

**T**he eighteenth century forerunners clad in hobnailed shoes or "tricounis" (special shoes equipped with pieces of metal on the sole) and today's climbers in slippers and fluorescent shorts are worlds apart. Not only is the equipment different but also the philosophy of mountaineering itself. Schematically, we can distinguish four big centres of attraction.

## On foot...

To hike, you only need a pair of shoes. Hiking can be done in very different ways. You can leave, lightly loaded, for a small hour on one of Flégère's trails but you can also walk for hundreds of kilometres around Mont Blanc with a twenty kilo rucksack on your back. Although the material differs somewhat, the aim of the game is the same: discover the mountain while quietly walking without having to venture in tricky spots.

Glaciers, rocky ledges, snow ridges and couloirs. Such are precisely the favourite playgrounds of mountaineers. The difference with hiking? Essentially the equipment and the technical difficulty. You don't mountaineer without ropes, ice axes, harnesses, pegs, crampons, etc. Nor without a minimum of knowledge of the high mountain's very particular conditions (weather forecast, relief, belaying techniques, etc.). Above all, walking is not the only thing: one must also climb, in short hang to the mountain with one's feet, hands... and the rest. Mountaineering routes are rated according to their difficulty (gradient, height, commitment, efforts, etc.) from "easy" to "exceptionally difficult". For information only, the Frendo route you've seen going up to Aiguille du Midi is rated "difficult".

## ... and with one's bare hands

A few years ago, people confused mountaineering and climbing. But today, the latter has won acclaim, notably with the success of Patrick Edlinger's movies. Unlike the mountaineer who walks (and eventually crosses glaciers) before reaching the foot of the actual

*Modern equipment (here an ice axe and crampons) has enabled the conquest of new and more difficult faces and routes.*

climbing route, the climber is only interested in the route itself and by the play between his body and the rock. Hence the success of the routes recently opened on the south face of Aiguille du Midi which don't require long approaches. The climber's material is lighter than the mountaineer's since crampons and ice axes are often not needed, whereas warm clothes and bivouac gear are generally not necessary because such climbs are done within a day.

Finally, we must not forget winter in the mountains. There also, things have changed. Consider all the new skiing techniques: alpine, cross-country, trekking, off-trail, extreme, monoski, snowsurf and even ski-mountaineering. In the high mountain of the Mont-Blanc massif, one mostly encounters skiing trekkers. The Vallée-Blanche ski descent is one of the many routes whose access is made easier by the Aiguille du Midi's cableway.

## The flying men

In the last ten years, new mountain sports were born: paragliding, mountain-biking, canyoning, hydro-speeding and hang-gliding. To paragliders Aiguille du Midi provides unique and gorgeous flights. The summit is a rather tricky take-off point but Plan de l'Aiguille is very much frequented. The paragliders land in the valley at the Chamonix Sports Centre. This attraction is a must.

# AIGUILLE DU MIDI'S GREATEST MOUNTAINEERING ROUTES

I n a little more than a century, Aiguille du Midi has seen thousands of mountaineers on all its faces. Many have tried to go down in legend by signing a first on the highest of the Aiguilles de Chamonix. The normal route, on the south-east face, was opened up as soon as 1869 and is still today very much used. Thus, if you see someone taking the snow ridge in line with the ice tunnel without skis, there's a strong chance he's going to the base of that face. This side of the peak has at least three important routes: the classic one, opened up for the first time in 1956 by two of the great names of mountaineering (the actor and cello player Maurice Baquet and the guide Gaston Rébuffat), the right pillar (Contamine route) and the direct route "Ma Dalton", the most difficult of Aiguille du Midi, opened up recently (1984) by two of today's best climbers: Gérard Hopfgartner and Michel Piola. More on the left on the south face is another route for modern high altitude climbing, "La dame du lac", opened by Gaetano and Romain Vogler in 1982.

## From Les Cosmiques to the north face

The Cosmiques spur which leads to a refuge bearing the same name (alpine glaciology laboratory) has two routes. The classic one, ("The Rebuffat") was opened up by the Chamonix guide accompanied by Bernard Pierre in 1956. As for the Cosmiques ridge, a short mixed run very much frequented today, it was first climbed as soon as 1911. Mountaineers taking this route come out of it by a small ladder at the Mont-Blanc terrace.

Finally, we must not forget to mention the north face which you first see when arriving by the cable car. It is the most spectacular and count Ferdinand de Bouillé though it "unassailable". It was climbed for the first time in 1879 and has today more than ten routes including the famous Frendo and Seigneur spurs.

■ **FIRE ON ICE**
During Aiguille du Midi's first ascent, count Ferdinand de Bouillé spent the night of the 4th to the 5th of August 1856 "3 500 metres above sea level at a temperature of ten degrees." He thus related his bivouac in the Vallée Blanche: "We stabbed our sticks in a circle and tied around it a sheet we had brought as well as my plaid... In the middle, we lit three logs as a makeshift fireplace... All the eleven of us gathered around the fire, a fire we had to move around all the time since it sunk in the snow producing more smoke than heat."

# BEHIND THE SCENES OF THE CABLEWAY

**T**he everyday running of the Aiguille du Midi's cableway requires a real entreprise employing more than forty people in high season: electricians, electronics engineers, mechanics, computer scientists, cashiers, car attendants and others working at the reception, exploitation, maintenance, administration, restaurants, etc. Most are from the Chamonix valley and its surroundings and all are perfectly familiar with the mountain.

## The mountain's wardens

All year long, rain or shine, two wardens alternatively spend the night at the summit for security reasons. Their role: make sure that all the visitors have gone down and start the generators in case of a power failure. Indeed, all the Aiguille du Midi's facilities (heating, lighting, kitchens, cableway, television transmitter) are electrically operated. The drinking water is brought in tanks by the cars. In summer, some two to three cubic meters of water are drank each day. For the everyday upkeep (toilets, floor cleaning, etc.) the snow melting from the roofs is collected in a twenty-five-thousand-litre tank which also provides a safety water supply in case of a fire.

## Cableway figures

|  | 1st section | 2nd section |
| --- | --- | --- |
| Altitude of the downhill station | 1 040 m | 2 317 m |
| Difference in height | 1 277 m | 1 461 m |
| Altitude of the uphill station | 2 317 m | 3 778 m |
| Length | 2 523 m | 2 869 m |
| Number of pylons | Three | None |
| Weight transported /car | 5 060 kg | 4 620 kg |
| Maximum speed | 36 km/hr | 45 km/hr |
| Number of passengers/car | 72 | 66 |
| Hourly passenger flow | 600 | 600 |
| Traction cable diameter | 40 mm | 40 mm |
| Suspension cable diameter | 52 mm | 52 mm |
| Transportations time | 8 minutes | 8 minutes |

# AIGUILLE DU MIDI'S PRACTICAL GUIDE

■ A CURIOUS PLANET
"Aiguille du Midi is probably
blessed by the gods. It's one
of our rare 'great' which can
be reached by cableway with
extreme climbers and
tourists in sandals rubbing
shoulders at its summit.
Rich, sumptuous,
paradoxical, it symbolises
man's desire for altitude. (...)
A very curious planet."
Jean-Mi Asselin

Renovated in 1991, the cableway is opened all year long except when the weather conditions are bad (very strong wind or heavy snowfalls). For information only: from 6 a.m. to 5 p.m. in July and August; from 8 a.m. to 4.45 p.m. in May, June and September; and from 8 a.m. to 3.45 p.m. the rest of the year (opening at 7 a.m. on week-ends and holidays when the Vallée-Blanche ski descent is possible). The cars leave every ten to thirty minutes.

In the high season (from February 1st to May 15th and from July 1st to August 31st) we advise you to reserve your place by telephone (50.53.40.00 twenty-four hours a day). You can make your booking as much as ten days in advance. Your reservations and tickets can be picked up and paid (cash, checks, American Express or Visa cards, traveller checks, deutschmarks, dollars, Swiss francs, liras, pounds and yens) on the site, at least one hour before the departure. Half the places in each car are however reservation-free. Along with your ticket, you will receive a boarding card specifying your car number (also displayed on the lighted sign in front of the station). Both should be presented to the controller. The cashier will also give you a departure time. Be present at least 10 minutes before boarding. If you're going to Italy, don't forget to bring along identity papers to cross the frontier. The Helbronner peak cable car runs from March to September. It enables you to make a fantastic excursion in one full day. From Chamonix back to Chamonix: going up to Plan de l'Aiguille (2 317 m) and Aiguille du Midi (3 778 and 3 842 m), flying over the Vallée Blanche and the Géant glaciers, arriving at the Helbronner peak (3 466 m) and going down to the Torino refuge (3 350 m), the Pavillon (2 130 m) and finally to La Palud-Courmayeur (1 325 m). From there, you return to Chamonix (1 030 m) by bus via the Mont-Blanc tunnel.

## Hikes

If you like to walk, you can also do the following run: take the cableway to Plan de l'Aiguille and Aiguille du

Midi, visit, return to Plan de l'Aiguille and walk back to Chamonix in two hours by the marked out trails of the Blaitière mountain. Good walking shoes are recommended and you may encounter some névés early in the season. Similarly, an alternative route enables you to reach the Mer de Glace (1 913 m) in a little over two hours. From there, you can return to Chamonix in less than two hours or take the small train of Montenvers. Even if the weather in the valley is beautiful, don't leave for Aiguille du Midi without warm clothing, essential at this altitude where the chilliness combined to a small breeze can considerably cool down the atmosphere. The temperature at the summit rarely goes over 0 °C and commonly goes down to – 10 °C. Sunglasses are also a must because of the intense reflection of the sun's radiance on the glaciers. Finally, because of the oxygen rarefaction at 3 800 m, the trip is not recommended to children under two and to people with heart problems. Although the site has been conceived to let you safely enjoy the sensations of the high mountain, don't forget that you are in a very special universe. Therefore, don't venture outside of the terraces nor on the slope that goes down towards the Vallée-Blanche itinerary.

*The moundain is a paradise for all kinds of mountaineers. There is a stroll, a hike or an altitude route for everyone.*

## Life in the great outdoors

If the great outdoors whet your appetite, several restaurants are opened: "Le 3 842" a traditional restaurant with a warm atmosphere has a seating capacity of thirty, the cafeteria (self-service) and two "Croque-minute" offering refreshments and fast-food service (see the plan on pages 18 and 19). At the summit, the most beautiful light is that of the sun rising over the Alps. To enjoy it, board early between 7 and 8 a.m. just after the first cars taken by the mountaineers. When you return follow the green signs saying Chamonix which will bring you back to the north peak and the departure station. On days of large crowds, boarding cards are also given for the return. You can pick them up as soon as you arrive at the information booth near the footbridge.

## Duration of the trip

(transportation time and visit included) :

| Starting from Chamonix | One-way trip | Round trip | Round trip in high season |
|---|---|---|---|
| Plan de l'Aiguille | 10 min | 1 hr | 1 hr 30 min |
| Aiguille du Midi | 20 min | 2 hr | 3 to 4 hr |
| Helbronner peak | 1 hr | 3 to 4 hr | 4 to 6 hr |
| La Palud-Courmayeur | 1 hr 40 min | | |

Inquiries : tel. 50.53.30.80.

SOCIETE TOURISTIQUE DU MONT-BLANC

*Right-hand page:*
*Mont Blanc as seen from*
*Aiguille du Midi.*

# THE VALLÉE-BLANCHE CABLE-CAR: A TREMENDOUS TECHNOLOGICAL CHALLENGE

■ A TRIBUTE
"Mont Blanc is a light cathedral with its pillars and its stained-glass windows. A closed cathedral of whom we only know the outside. Up there, we are confronted with simple elements: clouds, sun, snow, etc. And each time, I have the feeling of a new birth".
**Patrick Gabarrou**

When they finished building the Aiguille du Midi's cableway, count Dino Lora Totino di Cervinia and Philippe-Edmond Desailloud looked south-eastward in the direction of Italy. Once more their idea seems crazy: to link the Aoste and Chamonix valleys by striding over the mountain. Once more the nature of the ground calls for audacious technical choices. Indeed, to reach the Helbronner peak (3 466 m) where the Italian cableway (whose construction was completed in 1946) arrives, one must "fly over" two moving glaciers (the Vallée Blanche and the Géant). Five kilometres of living matter over which it is obviously impossible to lay down a single pylon...

## An absolutely unique technique

Between both summits, only Le Gros Rognon (3 541 m), a rock lost in the middle of ices and seracs, can serve as an anchorage point. But this single support is not enough and the technicians are forced to imagine a solution still unique in the world today: the construction of a pylon hanging by cables between the Petit Flambeau and Grand Flambeau (3 421 and 3 557 m) peaks four hundred and fifty metres from Helbronner. Opened in 1958, the Vallée-Blanche cable-car is composed of twelve 3-cartrains, each car carrying four passengers. The crossing of this startling landscape of crevasses and seracs lasts about twenty minutes at a speed of 3 m/sec (about 11 km/hr). A third of Aiguille du Midi's visitors continue to the Helbronner peak and some even go down to Courmayeur. With its passenger flow of one hundred and fifty per hour, the cable-car could not carry more people anyway. Now that the Aiguille du Midi's cableway has been renovated, a modernization of the cable-car is under consideration.

## Skiers seen from the sky

The Vallée-Blanche cable-car runs from March-April to September when the weather conditions are good (sometimes the wind scours the glaciers at more than two hundred kilometres an hour making the facilities unworkable). During the journey, your car will slow down and stop several times in order to board other passengers at the station. This is the time to take some pictures (the side windows can open) but be careful not to move around in the car. On the route you will also see the Vallée-Blanche ski descent. On a nice spring morning you will probably see some groups of skiers led by guides. After crossing Le Gros Rognon, the rocky east face of Mont Blanc du Tacul will appear on the right followed by the Aiguilles du Diable (4 144 m), Le Grand Capucin (3 838 m) and La Tour Ronde (3 992 m). On your left, the two slender peaks emerging before the arrival in Italy are Aiguille Noire (3402 m) and La Dent du Géant (4 013 m).

*The Vallée Blanche cable-car: a trip over a seracs nest.*

# FOLLOW THE GUIDE IN THE VALLÉE BLANCHE SKI DESCENT

*Les Grandes Jorasses as seen from the tunnel leading to the Vallée Blanche ski descent.*

The Vallée Blanche. This river, apparently stilted by the cold, has its source on the Mont Blanc du Tacul's slopes. It flows under Aiguille du Midi to end 14 kilometers lower down beyond the rocky ridge, called Les flammes de Pierre, in the extension of Les Drus. The Vallée Blanche is an off-trail skier's paradise, offering a long descent without a previous alpine mountains. From Aiguille du Midi, you tower above the fantastic universe of the high mountain. The Vallée Blanche leads you straight into its heart.

The route begins at the station of arrival of the second section of the cableway. When you reach the central peak, you take the ice tunnel to your left leading to a snowy ridge. Be careful ! The ridge and the glacier are dangerous and can only be taken by mountaineers carrying the required safety equipment.

## Unforgettable

A little after Le Gros Rognon, you can enjoy a first order view on the Brenva ridge, La Tour Ronde and the Aiguille du Diable below Mont Blanc du Tacul. After the Géant's seracs and the Requin refuge on your left, you will cross the Périades glacier on your right below the Rochefort ridges in the continuation of Les Grandes Jorasses.

Further down, the Leschaux glacier gives access to the north face of Les Grandes Jorasses in the background and to Aiguille du Moine via the Couvercle refuge. It emerges at a place called Salle à Manger under the protection of the Envers des Aiguilles (Grand Charmoz, Grépon, Blaitière, Fou...), and its refuge. Below, on your right, you can see Les Drus and Aiguille Verte (4 122 m).

You reach the end of an almost unreal journey crossing settings where some of the most beautiful chapters in the history of mountaineering have been written.

*Right-hand page: The Vallée Blanche, a very busy route in fine weather. Caution: high mountain.*

# THE MONT-BLANC TRAMWAY

■ **IN DAYS OF OLD...**
In 1909, the French alpine club magazine *Montagne et Alpinisme* wrote about the M.B.T. : " And now, one will be able to leave Paris at the end of the day, arrive for breakfast at the Voza pass, pick up (...) rhododendrons, (...) have a long look at the Aiguilles de Chamonix and Mont Blanc, think about the harsh but healthy efforts of yester year along these slopes and, three hours after one's arrival, take the train and be back in Paris the following morning."

**L**ong before the construction of the Aiguille du Midi's cableway and the Vallée-Blanche cable-car, another great human adventure took place in the Mont Blanc surroundings. Early in the century, Henri Duportal proposed a plan to get to the roof of Europe by a... railway to Aiguille du Goûter (3 863 m). From there an horizontal tunnel would have been dug all the way to the summit and Mont Blanc would have been reached... by lift !

## Anne, Jeanne and Marie

The work starts in December 1905 under the leadership of three engineers who had distinguished themselves in the Suez canal's construction. Six years later, the Mont-Blanc Tramway (M.B.T.) arrives at the Mont Lachat pass (2 073 m). However, subsequent technical and financial difficulties slow down the construction. World War I puts a final stop at the work and the M.B.T. is halted at Nid d'Aigle (2 372 m). At the time, more than five hours (half of that today) are needed to make the round trip because steam engines are used. One of them can still be seen at the Fayet station. The line is electrified in

1955 only. Three electric railcars still running today are then named Anne, Jeanne and Marie in honour of the daughters of the company's director. Additional equipment includes three trailer cars, a pushed snow plough and a snow reamer to clear the way in winter. Indeed the M.B.T. runs all year long with up to twelve trains a day in high season.

## M.B.T. figures

|  | Steam engines | Electric engines |
| --- | --- | --- |
| Speed | 8 km/hr | 20 km/hr |
| Weight when empty | 13.6 tons | 32 tons |
| Weigh when full | 27.3 tons | 39 tons |
| Water | 2 800 l | |
| Coal | 500 kg | |
| Tension of the network | | 11 000 V |
| Engine power | 200 h.p. | 640 h.p. |
| Seating capacity of each car | 55 | 59 |

In one full train, the M.B.T. can carry up to two hundred and twenty people.

*The Mont-Blanc tramway's arrival at Nid d'Aigle (2 372 m).*

# FOLLOW THE GUIDE TO NID D'AIGLE

**A**ll along its journey, the Mont-Blanc Tramway (M.B.T.) will make you discover the various levels of alpine vegetation to the slow rhythm of a small traditional mountain train. A little over twelve kilometres travelled in one hour and a quarter (the mean speed is 15 km/hr) which will bring you from Fayet (584 m) to Nid d'Aigle (2 372 m) at the foot of Aiguille du Goûter (3 863 m) and only a minute away from the Bionnassay glacier. The overall difference in height (1 788 m) is the largest in France.

## A hamlet miles from anywhere

The rails quickly leave the urban traffic, pass along the hydropathic establishments gardens, cross two or three small roads and reach the Saint-Gervais-les-Bains station. The few houses scattered here and there in the landscape may seem a little lop-sided to you. That's because the M.B.T. enters the most sloping part of its itinerary. Thanks to a rack placed in the middle of the railway for some ten kilometres, it can climb slopes up to 24%. Soon the chalets leave their place to a coniferous forest which lets you catch a glimpse of Mont Joly (2 525 m), the Bettex (1 350 m) and its ski-runs on the right and of the Aravis range in the background.

The third stop is at Montivon, a minuscule hamlet of the Saint-Gervais area which can only be reached by the M.B.T. in winter. The journey continues in the forest with some nice glimpses of the Contamine-Montjoie valley and the Bonhomme pass. A few minutes after the departure from Montivon, here is probably the nicest view on the village, Aiguille de Bionnassay and its glacier and on the left, Aiguille du Goûter and its glacier. But it's mostly when you come back in the evening that the landscape appears in all its finery under the setting sun.

## A glaciated terminus

At 1 653 m above sea level, the Voza pass marks the beginning of high mountain pastures and welcomes cow herds from Les Houches at the end of the summer. A more open landscape which will make you discover the Fiz range and the village of Servoz on the left as well as the Aiguilles-Rouges massif and the Brévent ski resort. Further on the right, Aiguille du Midi (3 842 m), Mont Blanc du Tacul (4 248 m) and Mont Blanc (4 807 m) tower over the town of Chamonix.

At Bellevue, the pastures sometimes make way for rhododendrons. This is the alpine level and the high mountain is not very far away. After the Mont Lachat pass (2 073 m), the mineral world inhabited by ibexes and marmots will gradually replace the vegetal one. The tramway must take two tunnels to drive round the Rognes rocky ridge and reach Nid d'Aigle. Not everybody stops here since many mountaineers continue towards the Tête-Rousse (3 167 m) and Aiguille-du-Goûter (3 817 m) refuges to finally reach the roof of Europe.

*The Tête-Rousse refuge,*
*three hours from Nid d'Aigle.*

# AUGUST 1786 : MONT-BLANC'S FIRST ASCENT

■ At de Saussure's request, the Swiss painter and etcher Marquard Wocher (1760-1830) will make the two etchings immortalizing his trip to Mont Blanc's summit in 1787, one year after the first ascent. These prints are now republished in the Hickory collection (right-hand page).

*Right-hand page: The 1787 etching depicting Horace-Bénédict de Saussure and Jacques Balmat coming down from Mont Blanc.*

Imagine the way mountaineers were equipped more than two hundred years ago : no ice axes, no light synthetic ropes, no waterproof shoes and with heavy uncomfortable clothes. Mont Blanc's first ascent is thus an authentic historical feat. In 1760, the Genevan academician Horace-Bénédict de Saussure is barely twenty years old when he discovers Mont Blanc while making herbariums. It proves to be a revelation. A few years later, he offers a prize for the discovery of a practicable route to the summit. But it's a hard task since none of the Chamonix guides wants to spend a night on the mountain. Too dangerous, they think. Almost by accident, but also because of the lure of gain, Jacques Balmat, a crystal and gold seeker, discovers that the thing is possible when he is trapped on a foggy day near Aiguille du Goûter.

## For the sake of Science

Having heard of his misadventure Michel-Gabriel Paccard, a doctor from Chamonix, hires him to try and reach the summit in exchange for Saussure's reward. It's a deal: with their rucksacks and their long staffs they leave a few days later for the mountain of La Côte where they bivouac. The following day, they cross Le Grand Plateau and Les Rochers Rouges to finally reach the Bosses ridge. At 6.23 p.m. on August 8th 1786 they reach the summit. They return to Chamonix the next day after another night on the glacier.

Informed by Jacques Balmat that the first ascent was lost on him (and that the reward had to be paid) Horace-Bénédict de Saussure will get to the summit only a year later. The scientist is then 47 years old and he will remain many hours at the summit to measure the altitude with the help of various barometers and to perform a whole series of experiments.

# FOLLOW THE GUIDE TO THE SUMMIT OF MONT BLANC

**M**ont Blanc embodies the purity of eternal snow. It symbolizes pride, consistency, certainty. It is the highest and makes you aware of it, inviting you to the journey and enticing you by the roundess of its attractive shapes.

As the saying has it, Mont Blanc is an easy mountain without any real technical difficulties for symbol seeking mountaineers. This appearance lures more than 23 000 poorly trained contenders a year on its slopes to better stop them, out of breath and of dreams, bent over their ice axes and startled by the realisation that altitude itself is a big enough obstacle. Although many don't reach the summit, some 12 000 to 13 000 succeed and get to stare, wild with joy, at the whole world at their feet.

The Société Touristique du Mont-Blanc (S.T.M.B.) plays an important role in the conquest of Mont Blanc. Thus, the Mont-Blanc tramway leads to the starting point for the Tête-Rousse and Goûter refuges and the Aiguille du Midi cableway leads to Les Grands Mulets via Plan de l'Aiguille and Les Cosmiques via Aiguille du Midi's summit.

## The exhilaration of the summit

Most contenders start by the Mont-Blanc tramway. From Nid d'Aigle, they climb a rocky path broken with névés first to the Tête Rousse (2 372 m) and then to the Goûter (3 817 m) refuges. Although the walk up to Tête Rousse is rather easy (caution: it requires good shoes, has a 800 m difference in height and is often snow-covered) the rest of the journey is less so.

After Tête Rousse, you must climb the left bank of the glacier up to the foot of the first rocky escarpments where you will have to cross the great snowslide coming down from Aiguille du Goûter's summit. A cable has been installed to make the crossing easier but the slope is very steep and rocks frequently fall from the summit. Then, a very abrupt route brings you to the Goûter refuge. There, still no Mont Blanc in sight ! You will have to get up early and climb to

Dôme du Goûter (4 304 m) to finally see it. Afterwards, the normal route goes down to the Dôme pass (4 237 m) and up to the Vallot refuge (4 362 m). From there, you will have to take the Brosses ridge (Grande Bosse: 4 513 m and Petite Bosse: 4 677 m) to reach the summit. Your feelings at the summit are very personal. The beauty, the silence and this particular light welcoming you leave an indelible mark on your mind and each summit renews the magic.

Listen to Patrick Gabarrou who opened a hundredth routes in the Mont Blanc massif: *"Mont Blanc is like a dream space: I have only brushed at something I could not grasp. Like a woman you kiss but is never yours."*

# A MOUNTAIN OF RECORDS

From time immemorial, Mont Blanc has given rise to the wildest adventures. The guide René Claret-Tournier, having climbed more than five hundred times the normal route since 1947 (thirty-six times in the same year !), holds the record of records, the others varying from true to "cranky" feats.

## From 8 to 84 years old

In the first category, one must quote the ascent of the 84 year old guide Ulrich Imberden in 1985. In 1890, the 71 year old scientist Jules Janssen did arrive to the summit but in a sleigh pulled by eight guides. The youngest mountaineer to reach the summit was 8 year old Cristel Bochatay in 1975, the Goûter refuge warden's daughter.

Although Horace-Bénédict de Saussure was the instigator of the first ascent in 1786, he reached the summit the following year only and measured its altitude at 4 775 m, making an insignificant error considering the means of the time. In 1887 Joseph Vallot spent three nights at the summit, three years before building the first refuge-observatory on the Bosses ridge. In 1938 a couple spent a week under an igloo. But the longest stay is probably that of two astronomers from the Janssen observatory in 1905: fifteen days.

## Always faster

Some prefer to go for the speed. Thus the first ratified record time for the Chamonix-Mont-Blanc round trip is 15 hrs 55 min in... 1864 ! A number which will evolve from 13 hrs (by night !) in 1910 to 8 hrs 10 min 20 sec in 1975.

Other record times: the classic hike round Mont-Blanc in 21 hrs 40 min and a Genève-Mont-Blanc in 21 hrs 30 min !

# MONT BLANC'S PRACTICAL GUIDE

■ **POPE**
**On September 7th 1986, Pope Jean-Paul II, keen on mountain hiking, came to the Mont-Blanc massif by the Helbronner peak cableway to celebrate the first ascent's bicentennial. However, he was not the first pope at that altitude. Indeed, Pie XI has done better in 1890 when, together with Bonin, he opened the normal climbing route from Courmayeur. But at the time his name was only Ratti, since he became a pope only in 1922.**

## Tourist offices :

Chamonix. Tel.: 50.53.00.24.
Courmayeur. Tel.: 19.39.165.84.20.60.
Les Contamines-Montjoie. Tel.: 50.47.01.58.
Les Houches. Tel.: 50.55.50.62.
Saint-Gervais. Tel.: 50.78.22.43.

## Société Touristique du Mont-Blanc:

Aiguille-du-Midi cableway. Tel.: 50.33.30.80.
Vallée-Blanche cable-car. Tel.:50.53.30.80.
Brévent cable-car. Tel.: 50.53.13.18.
Mont-Blanc Tramway (Saint-Gervais). Tel.: 50.47.51.83.

## Refuges:

Aiguille-du-Goûter (French alpine club, 3 817 m). Tel.: 50.54.40.93.
Le Requin (French alpine club, 2 516 m). Tel.: 50.53.16.96.
Les Cosmiques (Chamonix guides company, 3 613 m). Tel.: 50.54.40.16.
Les Grands-Mulets (French alpine club, 3 051 m). Tel.: 50.53.16.98.
Tête-Rousse (French alpine club, 3 167 m). Tel.: 50.58.24.97.
Torino (Italian alpine club, 3 330 m). Tel.: 19.39.165.84.22.47.

## Guide companies:

Chamonix. Tel.: 50.53.00.88.
Courmayeur. Tel.: 19.39.165.84.20.64.
Freelance guides. Tel.: 50.53.27.05.
Saint-Gervais. Tel.: 50.78.35.37.

*Preceding page:
A solitary climb by Jean-Christophe Lafaille, opening a new route on the Freney on the Italian side of Mont Blanc.*

*Right-hand page:
Aiguille du Midi and the snow ridge leading to the Vallée Blanche.*

## Miscellaneous:

Police and mountain assistance. Tel.: 50.53.16.89.
Chamonix weather forecast. Tel.: 50.53.03.40.

# THE SOCIÉTÉ TOURISTIQUE DU MONT-BLANC

■ **CONTACTS**
**Aiguille du Midi's cableway.**
**Tel.: 50.53.30.80.**
**Vallée-Blanche cable-car.**
**Tel.: 50.53.30.80.**
**Brévent cable car (ski resort**
**and climbing routes).**
**Tel.: 50.53.13.18.**
**Mont-Blanc Tramway**
**(Saint-Gervais).**
**Tel.: 50.47.51.83.**
**Sogertam Restauration.**
**Tel.: 50.53.30.80.**
**La Tour-Balme**
**(SETA, ski resort and hikes).**
**Tel.: 50.54.00.58.**

The Société Touristique du Mont-Blanc (STMB), a limited company with a 23 760 000 franc capital is one of the few French mountain enterprises to have a Stock Exchange rating, the public holding 24% of the shares. The majority belongs to PLM (the Wagons-lits group) a firm associated for a long time with the Chamonix way of life thanks to the railway link between Paris and the mountaineering's capital.

## For the love of the mountain

In addition to the Aiguille du Midi's cableway, the Vallée-Blanche cable-car, the Brévent cable-car and ski resort and the Mont-Blanc Tramway, the S.T.M.B. also manages the Tour-Balme ski lifts and resort (through its subsidiary, the SETA) as well as six restaurants (via another subsidiary, the SOGERTAM). Mountain transport thus remains the firm's main priority with particular emphasis on the quality of the reception and the visitors confort as well as the

*The S.T.M.B. team.*

constant improvement of the transport conditions thanks to the modernization of the facilities, etc. As a consequence, two hundred million francs were invested in the last six years (Aiguille du Midi's new buildings in 1985, Brévent's reconstruction in 1989, Tour-Balme resort equipment, Aiguille du Midi's cableway renovation in 1991). Future priorities include the Brévent-Flégère link, the Tour-Balme resort expansion towards Vallorcine and the Vallée-Blanche cable-car and Mont-Blanc Tramway renovation.

## Millions of visitors

Since the Aiguille du Midi's cableway construction, almost nine million people have had the opportunity to enter the fantastic universe of the high mountain. At present, Aiguille du Midi's summit welcomes some four hundred and fifty thousand visitors a year (about five thousand a day in high season). The S.T.M.B. receives about 1.2 million people on all its various facilities.

Société Touristique du Mont-Blanc, 100, parking de l'Aiguille du Midi, 74400 Chamonix.
Tel.: 50.53.30.80. Fax: 50.55.99.76.

**Photography**

Michel Ferrer : 22, 24 and 25, 28, 35, 43, 45. Philippe Poulet : 6, 8, 9, 10, 20 and 21, 26 and27, 34 (up), 36, 41, 44, 59. Xavier Murillo : cover, 46, 55, 61. Jeremy Balcam : 7, 11, 12 and 13, 23, 29, 30 and 31, 33, 48, 51, 56 and 57. STMB : 4, 43 (Mingasson), 15 (Dablanc), 17, 38, 49 (Bigart), 50, 53. Jean Kouchner : 34 (down), 54. Pascal Kober : 2 and 3.

© 1992 STMB - Thetys
All rights reserved
ISBN 2-9506949-1-8
Dépôt légal : août 1992
Conception and graphic work: LIBRIS/G. Parmentier
Printed in Spain.